Japan Surface Warships
2019 – 2020

Other books available on Amazon.com:

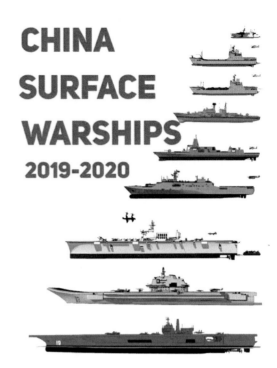

TABLE OF CONTENTS

Izumo Class Aircraft Carriers

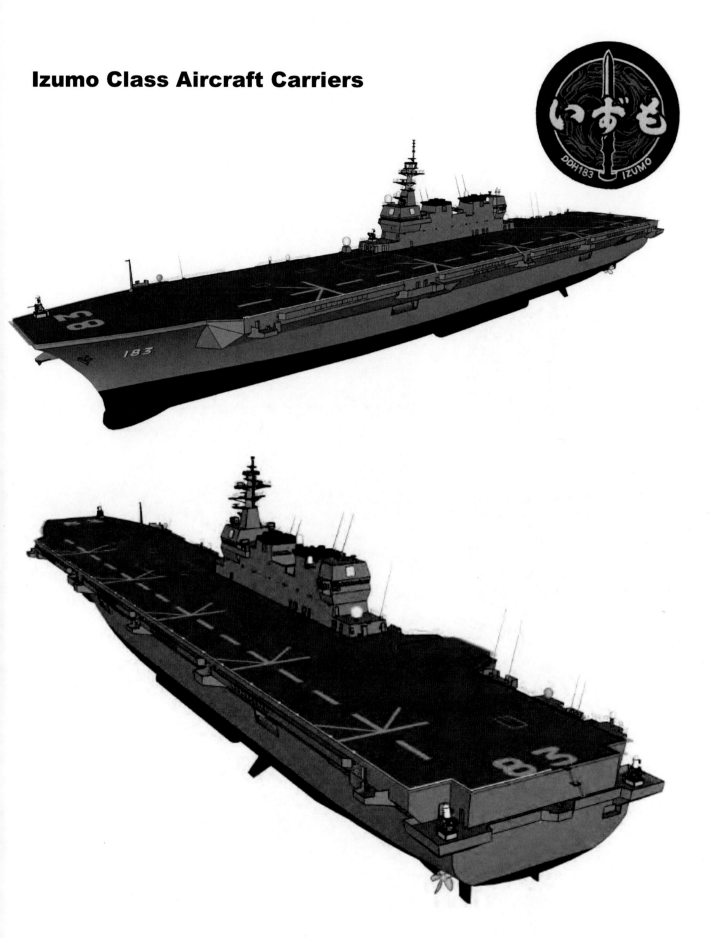

3D model by: Sir Topham hatt

DDH-183 JS Izumo Aircraft Carrier

海上自衛隊 / Japan Maritime Self-Defense Force

Japanese Name	いずも型護衛艦 Izumo-gata-goei-kan		
Type (Class)	Izumo-class multi-purpose destroyer		
Commissioned	2015		
Length (meters)	248	**Crew**	970 incl crew and troops
Width (meters)	38	**Speed** (knots)	30
Draft (meters)	7.5	**Range** (nmi)	
Displacement (tons)			
Standard	19,500	**Fully Loaded**	27,000
Propulsion	COGAG, two shafts		
	4 × GE/IHI LM2500IEC gas turbine		
Weapons	2 × Phalanx CIWS		
	2 × 11 SeaRAM missiles		
	2 × Triple 324mm torpedoes tubes		
Aircraft (28 max)	12 × F-35B Lightning II STOVL, 8 × V-22 Osprey,		
	8 × ASW and SAR helicopters or 14 larger aircraft		

In December 2018, the Japanese Cabinet gave approval to convert the DDH-183 JS Izumo and DDH-184 JS Kaga into aircraft carriers capable of operating the F-35B STOVL (short take-off vertical landing).

3D model by: Sir Topham hatt

Initial modifications are taking place during the refit and overhaul planned for this fiscal year to convert the Izumo-class into aircraft carrier with reinforcement of the decks including the stowage and elevators to support the additional weight of F-35B, as well as the heat and forces from the jets during vertical landing. Note that the ship was built with hangar elevators big enough to accommodate F-35B fighters. Other modifications include placing additional landing lights. Final changes are planned to be made during the vessel's next overhaul in FY 2025. It is highly unlikely to retrofit the ship with catapult systems due to their expense and below-deck space requirements. Without catapults, the Izumo will not be able to launch aircraft with heavy ordinance loads.

The Izumo can carry up to 28 aircraft including (12) F-35B, (8) V-22 Osprey tiltrotor aircraft and (8) ASW (Anti-Submarine Warfare) or SRA (Search And Rescue) helicopters, or (14) large aircraft. Only (7) ASW helicopters and (2) SAR helicopters are planned for the initial aircraft complement. For other operations, (400) troops and (50) 3.5-ton trucks (or equivalent equipment) can also be carried. The flight deck has (5) helicopter landing spots that allow simultaneous landings and take-offs.

DDH-184   JS Kaga Aircraft Carrier

Photo: Yamada Taro

Japanese Name	加賀国 Kaga no kuni		
Type (Class)	Izumo-class helicopter destroyer		
Commissioned	2017		
Length (meters)	248	**Crew**	970 incl crew and troops
Width (meters)	38	**Speed** (knots)	30
Draft (meters)	7.5	**Range** (nmi)	

Displacement (tons)

Standard	19,500	**Fully Loaded**	27,000
Propulsion	COGAG, two shafts		
	4 × GE/IHI LM2500IEC gas turbine		
Weapons	2 × Phalanx CIWS		
	2 × 11 SeaRAM missiles		
Aircraft (28 max)	2 × Triple 324mm torpedoes tubes		
	12 × F-35B Lightning II STOVL, 8 × V-22 Osprey,		
	8 × ASW and SAR helicopters or 14 larger aircraft		

Photo: Hunini

DDH-184   JS Kaga Aircraft Carrier

Hyūga Class Helicopter Destroyers

JMSDF DDH 181 HYUGA

3D model by: Rintaro3776

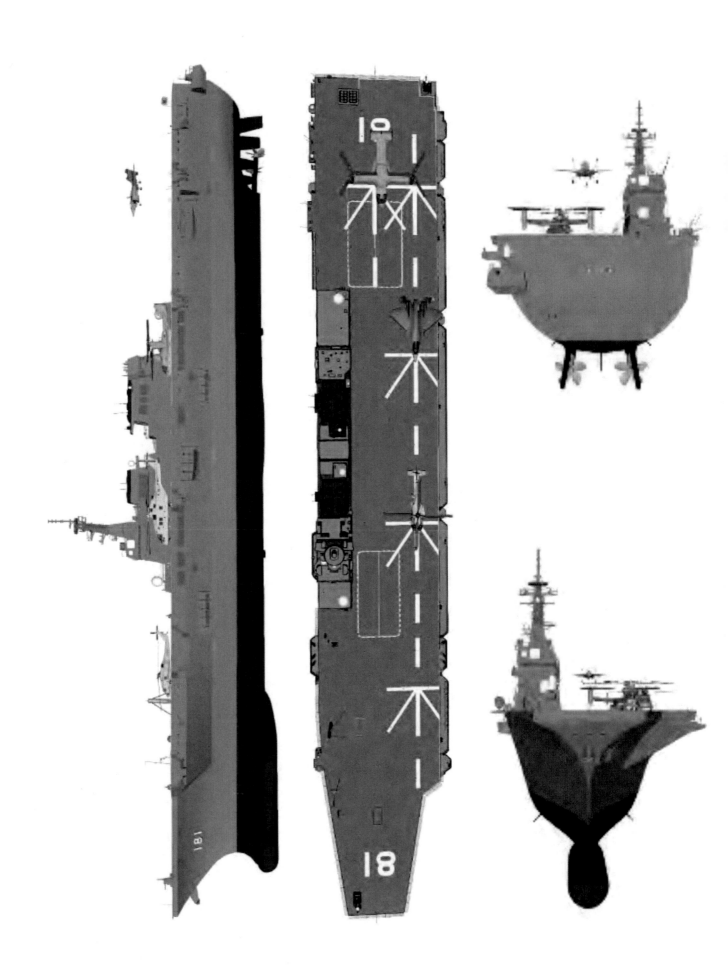

DDH-181   JS Hyūga Helicopter Destroyer

海上自衛隊 / Japan Maritime Self-Defense Force

Japanese Name ひゅうが型護衛艦 Hyūga-gata-goei-kan (護衛艦, lit. escort ship)
Type (Class) Hyūga-class helicopter destroyer
Commissioned   2009

Length (meters)	197	**Crew**	360
Width (meters)	33	**Speed** (knots)	30
Draft (meters)	7	**Range** (nmi)	

Displacement (tons)

Standard 19,500   **Fully Loaded** 27,000

Propulsion   COGAG, 4 × Ishikawajima Harima/General Electric LM2500-30 gas turbines
Two shafts 5-bladed CP props, 100,000 shaft horsepower (75 MW)

Weapons   16 cells Mk 41 VLS
16 ESSM
12 RUM-139 VL ASROC
2 × 20mm Phalanx CIWS
2 × triple 324mm torpedo tubes
12.7mm MG

Aircraft   3 × SH-60K Sea Hawk
1 × MCH-101 Airborne Mine Countermeasures (AMCM) helicopter
18 aircraft maximum

SH-60K Sea Hawk - Navy Photo By US Ensign Stephanie Krueger

MCH-101 Airborne Mine Countermeasures (AMCM) helicopter - 海上自衛隊

DDH-182   JS Ise Helicopter Destroyer

U.S. Navy photo by Lt. Cmdr. Denver Applehans

Japanese Name	伊勢		
Type (Class)	Hyūga-class helicopter destroyer		
Commissioned	2011		
Length (meters)	197	**Crew**	371
Width (meters)	33	**Speed** (knots)	30
Draft (meters)	7	**Range** (nmi)	
Displacement (tons)			
Standard	19,500	**Fully Loaded**	27,000
Propulsion	COGAG, 4 × Ishikawajima Harima/General Electric LM2500-30 gas turbines		
	Two shafts, 5-bladed CP props, 100,000 shaft horsepower (75 MW)		
Weapons	16 cells Mk 41 VLS		
	16 ESSM		
	12 RUM-139 VL ASROC		
	2 × 20mm Phalanx CIWS		
	2 × triple 324mm torpedo tubes		
	12.7mm MG		
Aircraft	3 × SH-60K Sea Hawk		
	1 × MCH-101 Airborne Mine Countermeasures (AMCM) helicopter		
	18 aircraft maximum		

JS Ise Launches Evolved Sea Sparrow
Missile during RIMPAC

DDH-182 JS Ise Helicopter Destroyer

Maya Class Guided Missile Destroyers

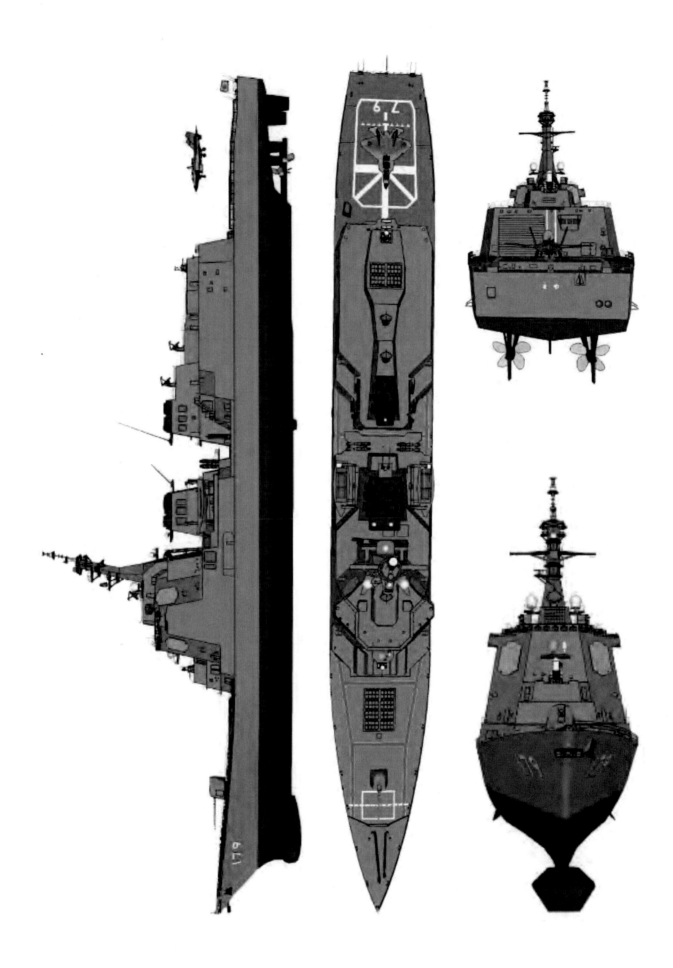

14

DDG-179 JS Maya Guided Missile Destroyer (Aegis)

Japanese Name	摩耶山 Maya-san		
Type (Class)	Maya-class guided missile destroyer (Aegis)		
Commissioned	2020		
Length (meters)	169.9	**Crew**	300
Width (meters)	22.2	**Speed** (knots)	30
Draft (meters)	6.4	**Range** (nmi)	
Displacement (tons)			
Standard	8,200	**Fully Loaded**	10,250

Propulsion 4 × IHI/General Electric LM2500-30 gas turbines
     Two shafts 5-bladed CP props, 68,010 shp (50.7 MW)

Weapons 1 × 5-inch (127mm/L62) Mk-45 Mod 4 naval gun in a stealth-shaped mount.
     2 × missile canister up to 8 Type 17
     2 × 20 mm Phalanx CIWS
     2 × Type 68 triple torpedo tubes (6 × Mk-46 or Type 73 torpedoes)
     96-cell Mk-41 VLS (64 at the bow / 32 cells at the stern aft) for a mix of:
      SM-2MR Standard Missile
      SM-3 Anti-Ballistic Missile
      SM-6 Standard Missile
      Type 07 VL-ASROC

Aircraft 1 × SH-60K Sea Hawk helicopter

DDG-180　JS Haguro Guided Missile Destroyer (Aegis)

By Hunini - Own work, CC BY-SA 4.0

Japanese Name	羽黒山 Haguro-san		
Type (Class)	Maya-class guided missile destroyer (Aegis)		
Commissioned	2021		
Length (meters)	169.9	**Crew**	300
Width (meters)	22.2	**Speed** (knots)	30
Draft (meters)	6.4	**Range** (nmi)	
Displacement (tons)			
Standard	8,200	**Fully Loaded**	10,250

Propulsion　　　4 × IHI/General Electric LM2500-30 gas turbines
　　　　　　　　　Two shafts 5-bladed CP props, 68,010 shp (50.7 MW)

Weapons　　　　1 × 5-inch (127mm/L62) Mk-45 Mod 4 naval gun in a stealth-shaped mount.
　　　　　　　　　2 × missile canister up to 8 Type 17
　　　　　　　　　2 × 20 mm Phalanx CIWS
　　　　　　　　　2 × Type 68 triple torpedo tubes (6 × Mk-46 or Type 73 torpedoes)
　　　　　　　　　96-cell Mk-41 VLS (64 at the bow / 32 cells at the stern aft) for a mix of:
　　　　　　　　　　SM-2MR Standard Missile
　　　　　　　　　　SM-3 Anti-Ballistic Missile
　　　　　　　　　　SM-6 Standard Missile
　　　　　　　　　　Type 07 VL-ASROC

Aircraft　　　　1 × SH-60K Sea Hawk helicopter

Atago-class Guided Missile Destroyer (Aegis)

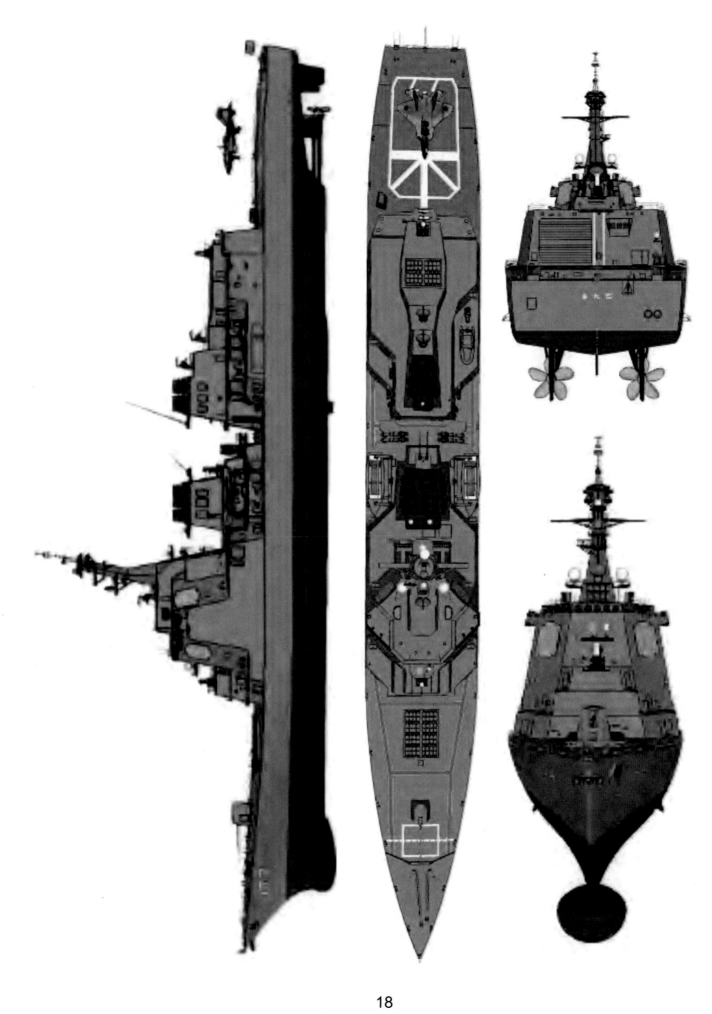

18

DD-177   JS Atago Guided Missile Destroyer (Aegis)

Photo: Jennifer A. Villalovos, U.S. Navy

Japanese Name	あたご A-ta-go		
Type (Class)	Atago-class guided missile destroyer (Aegis)		
Commissioned	2007		
Length (meters)	170	**Crew**	300
Width (meters)	21	**Speed** (knots)	30
Draft (meters)	6.2	**Range** (nmi)	4,500 at 20 knots

Displacement (tons)

Standard	7,700	**Fully Loaded**	10,000

Propulsion   4 × IHI/General Electric LM2500-30 gas turbines,
Two shafts, 100,000 shp (75 MW)

Weapons   1 × 5-inch (127mm/L62) Mk-45 Mod 4 naval gun in a stealth-shaped mount.
2 × missile canister up to 8 Type 90 (SSM-1B)
2 × 20 mm Phalanx CIWS
2 × Type 68 triple torpedo tubes (6 × Mk-46 or Type 73 torpedoes)
96-cell Mk-41 VLS (64 at the bow / 32 cells at the stern aft) for a mix of:
  SM-2MR Standard Missile
  SM-3 Anti-Ballistic Missile
  SM-6 Standard Missile
  RUM-139 Vertical Launch ASROC (Anti-Submarine)

Aircraft   1 × SH-60K Sea Hawk helicopter

DDG-178   JS Ashigara Guided Missile Destroyer (Aegis)

Photo: Veronica Mammina, U.S. Navy

Japanese Name	足柄山		
Type (Class)	Atago-class guided missile destroyer (Aegis)		
Commissioned	2008		
Length (meters)	170	**Crew**	300
Width (meters)	21	**Speed** (knots)	30
Draft (meters)	6.2	**Range** (nmi)	4,500 at 20 knots
Displacement (tons)			
Standard	7,700	**Fully Loaded**	10,000
Propulsion	4 × IHI/General Electric LM2500-30 gas turbines, Two shafts, 100,000 shp (75 MW)		
Weapons	1 × 5-inch (127mm/L62) Mk-45 Mod 4 naval gun in a stealth-shaped mount. 2 × missile canister up to 8 Type 90 (SSM-1B) 2 × 20 mm Phalanx CIWS 2 × Type 68 triple torpedo tubes (6 × Mk-46 or Type 73 torpedoes) 96-cell Mk-41 VLS (64 at the bow / 32 cells at the stern aft) for a mix of: SM-2MR Standard Missile SM-3 Anti-Ballistic Missile SM-6 Standard Missile RUM-139 Vertical Launch ASROC (Anti-Submarine)		
Aircraft	1 × SH-60K Sea Hawk helicopter		

Kongō-class Guided Missile Destroyers

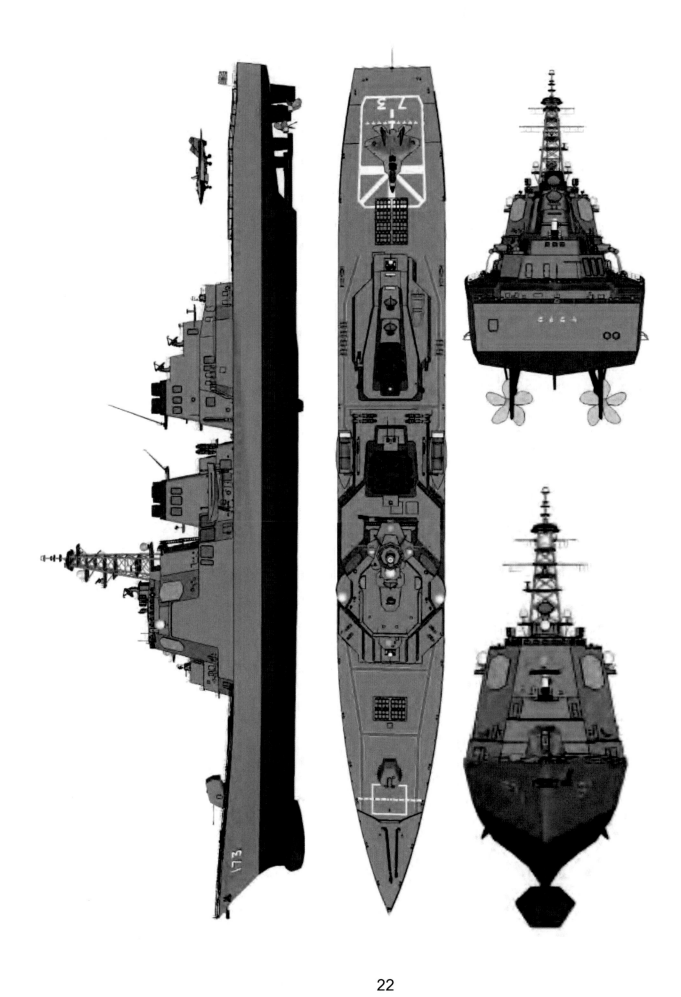

DDG-173 JS Kongō Guided Missile Destroyer (Aegis)

Photo: James E. Foehl, U.S. Navy

Japanese Name	金剛		
Type (Class)	Kongō-class guided missile destroyer (Aegis)		
Commissioned	1993		
Length (meters)	161	**Crew**	300
Width (meters)	21	**Speed** (knots)	30
Draft (meters)	6.2	**Range** (nmi)	4,500 at 20 knots

Displacement (tons)

Standard	7,500	**Fully Loaded**	9,500

Propulsion 4 × IHI/General Electric LM2500-30 gas turbines,
Two shafts, 100,000 shp (75 MW)

Weapons 1 × 5 inch (127 mm) / 54 caliber Oto-Breda Compact Gun
2 × missile canister up to 8 RGM-84 Harpoon SSM
2 × 20 mm Phalanx CIWS
2 × Type 68 triple torpedo tubes (6 × Mk-46 or Type 73 torpedoes)
90-cell Mk-41 VLS (29 at the bow / 61 cells at the stern aft) for a mix of:
 SM-2MR Standard Missile
 SM-3 Anti-Ballistic Missile
 RUM-139 Vertical Launch ASROC (Anti-Submarine)

Aircraft 1 × SH-60K Sea Hawk helicopter

DDG-174   JS Kirishima Guided Missile Destroyer (Aegis)

Photo: James G. Mccarter, U.S. Navy

Japanese Name	霧島山 Kirishimayama		
Type (Class)	Kongō-class guided missile destroyer (Aegis)		
Commissioned	1995		
Length (meters)	161	**Crew**	300
Width (meters)	21	**Speed** (knots)	30
Draft (meters)	6.2	**Range** (nmi)	4,500 at 20 knots

Displacement (tons)

Standard	7,500	**Fully Loaded**	9,500

Propulsion   4 × IHI/General Electric LM2500-30 gas turbines,
Two shafts, 100,000 shp (75 MW)

Weapons
1 × 5 inch (127 mm) / 54 caliber Oto-Breda Compact Gun
2 × missile canister up to 8 RGM-84 Harpoon SSM
2 × 20 mm Phalanx CIWS
2 × Type 68 triple torpedo tubes (6 × Mk-46 or Type 73 torpedoes)
90-cell Mk-41 VLS (29 at the bow / 61 cells at the stern aft) for a mix of:
  SM-2MR Standard Missile
  SM-3 Anti-Ballistic Missile
  RUM-139 Vertical Launch ASROC (Anti-Submarine)

Aircraft   1 × SH-60K Sea Hawk helicopter

An SM-3 (Block 1A) missile is launched from the
Japan Maritime Self-Defense Force destroyer JS Kirishima.

DDG-175   JS Myōkō Guided Missile Destroyer (Aegis)

Japanese Name	妙高山 Myōkō-san		
Type (Class)	Kongō-class guided missile destroyer (Aegis)		
Commissioned	1996		
Length (meters)	161	**Crew**	300
Width (meters)	21	**Speed** (knots)	30
Draft (meters)	6.2	**Range** (nmi)	4,500 at 20 knots

Displacement (tons)

Standard	7,500	**Fully Loaded**	9,500

Propulsion   4 × IHI/General Electric LM2500-30 gas turbines,
Two shafts, 100,000 shp (75 MW)

Weapons   1 × 5 inch (127 mm) / 54 caliber Oto-Breda Compact Gun
2 × missile canister up to 8 RGM-84 Harpoon SSM
2 × 20 mm Phalanx CIWS
2 × Type 68 triple torpedo tubes (6 × Mk-46 or Type 73 torpedoes)
90-cell Mk-41 VLS (29 at the bow / 61 cells at the stern aft) for a mix of:
 SM-2MR Standard Missile
 SM-3 Anti-Ballistic Missile
 RUM-139 Vertical Launch ASROC (Anti-Submarine)

Aircraft   1 × SH-60K Sea Hawk helicopter

DDG-176   JS Chōkai Guided Missile Destroyer (Aegis)

Photo: U.S. Navy

Japanese Name	鳥海山 Chōkai-san
Type (Class)	Kongō-class guided missile destroyer (Aegis)
Commissioned	1998

Length (meters)	161	**Crew**	300
Width (meters)	21	**Speed** (knots)	30
Draft (meters)	6.2	**Range** (nmi)	4,500 at 20 knots

Displacement (tons)

Standard	7,500	**Fully Loaded**	9,500

Propulsion   4 × IHI/General Electric LM2500-30 gas turbines,
Two shafts, 100,000 shp (75 MW)

Weapons   1 × 5 inch (127 mm) / 54 caliber Oto-Breda Compact Gun
2 × missile canister up to 8 RGM-84 Harpoon SSM
2 × 20 mm Phalanx CIWS
2 × Type 68 triple torpedo tubes (6 × Mk-46 or Type 73 torpedoes)
90-cell Mk-41 VLS (29 at the bow / 61 cells at the stern aft) for a mix of:
  SM-2MR Standard Missile
  SM-3 Anti-Ballistic Missile
  RUM-139 Vertical Launch ASROC (Anti-Submarine)

Aircraft   1 × SH-60K Sea Hawk helicopter

Hatakaze-Class Guided Missile Destroyers

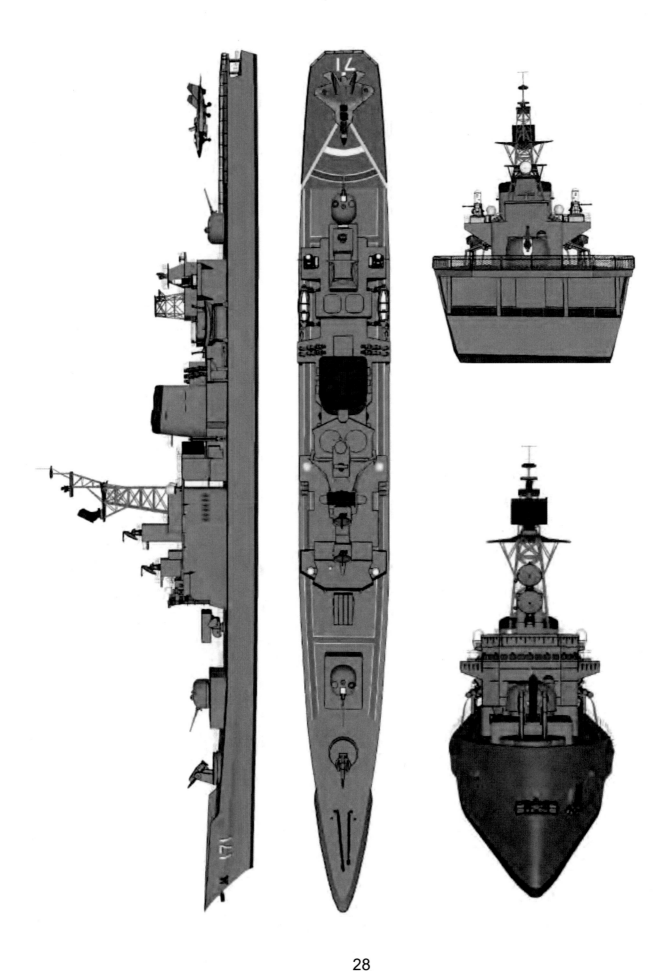

DDG-171 JS Hatakaze Guided Missile Destroyer

Photo: Benjamin Wooldridge, U. S. Navy

Japanese Name	ハタカゼ		
Type (Class)	Hatakaze-class guided missile destroyer		
Commissioned	1986		
Length (meters)	150	**Crew**	260
Width (meters)	16.4	**Speed** (knots)	30
Draft (meters)	4.8	**Range** (nmi)	4,500 at 20 knots
Displacement (tons)			
Standard	4,600	**Fully Loaded**	6,000
Propulsion	2 × Kawasaki Rolls-Royce Spey SM1A gas turbines for cruising 2 × Rolls-Royce Olympus gas turbines for high speed only, 72,000 hp (54 MW), 2 shafts		
Weapons	RGM-84 Harpoon SSM Standard missile MR SAM ASROC anti-submarine rocket 2 × 5-inch/54 caliber Mark 42 guns 2 × 20mm CIWS 2 × Type 68 triple torpedo tubes		
Aircraft	1 × SH-60K Sea Hawk helicopter		

DDG-172   JS Shimakaze Guided Missile Destroyer

Photo: U.S. Navy

Japanese Name	島風 (Island wind)		
Type (Class)	Hatakaze-class guided missile destroyer		
Commissioned	1986		
Length (meters)	150	**Crew**	260
Width (meters)	16.4	**Speed** (knots)	30
Draft (meters)	4.8	**Range** (nmi)	4,500 at 20 knots

Displacement (tons)

Standard	4,650	**Fully Loaded**	6,050

Propulsion   2 × Kawasaki Rolls-Royce Spey SM1A gas turbines for cruising
2 × Rolls-Royce Olympus gas turbines for high speed only,
72,000 hp (54 MW), 2 shafts

Weapons   RGM-84 Harpoon SSM
Standard missile MR SAM
ASROC anti-submarine rocket
2 × 5-inch/54 caliber Mark 42 guns
2 × 20mm CIWS
2 × Type 68 triple torpedo tubes

Aircraft   1 × SH-60K Sea Hawk helicopter

Asahi-Class Guided Missile Destroyers

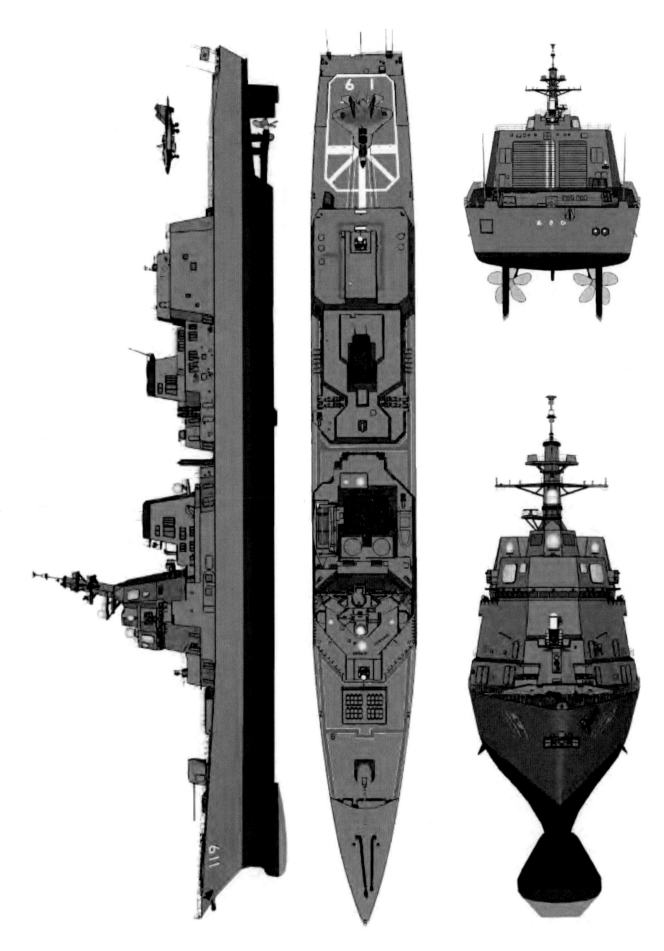

DD-119　JS Asahi Guided Missile Destroyer

Japanese Name	あさひ (Morning Sun)		
Type (Class)	Asahi-class guided missile destroyer		
Commissioned	Mar 2018		
Length (meters)	151	**Crew**	230
Width (meters)	18.3	**Speed** (knots)	30
Draft (meters)	5.4	**Range** (nmi)	4,500 at 20 knots

Displacement (tons)

Standard	5,100	**Fully Loaded**	6,800

Propulsion　COGLAG, two shafts, two GE LM2500 turbines

Weapons
8 × Type 90 SSM
1 × Mk 41 VLS (32cells)
RIM-162 ESSM SAM
RUM-139 VL-ASROC
Type 07 VL-ASROC
1 × 127 mm (5 in)/62 gun
2 × 20 mm Phalanx Block1B CIWS
2 × HOS-303 triple 324 mm (12.8 in) torpedo tubes

Aircraft　1 × SH-60K Sea Hawk helicopter

DD-120   JS Shiranui Guided Missile Destroyer

Japanese Name	不知火 (Phosphorescent Light)			
Type (Class)	Asahi-class guided missile destroyer			
Commissioned	Feb 2019			
Length (meters)	151	**Crew**	230	
Width (meters)	18.3	**Speed** (knots)	30	
Draft (meters)	5.4	**Range** (nmi)	4,500 at 20 knots	
Displacement (tons)				
Standard	5,100	**Fully Loaded**	6,800	
Propulsion	COGLAG, two shafts, two GE LM2500 turbines			
Weapons	8 × Type 90 SSM			
	1 × Mk 41 VLS (32cells)			
	RIM-162 ESSM SAM			
	RUM-139 VL-ASROC			
	Type 07 VL-ASROC			
	1 × 127 mm (5 in)/62 gun			
	2 × 20 mm Phalanx Block1B CIWS			
	2 × HOS-303 triple 324 mm (12.8 in) torpedo tubes			
Aircraft	1 × SH-60K Sea Hawk helicopter			

Akizuki-Class Guided Missile Destroyers

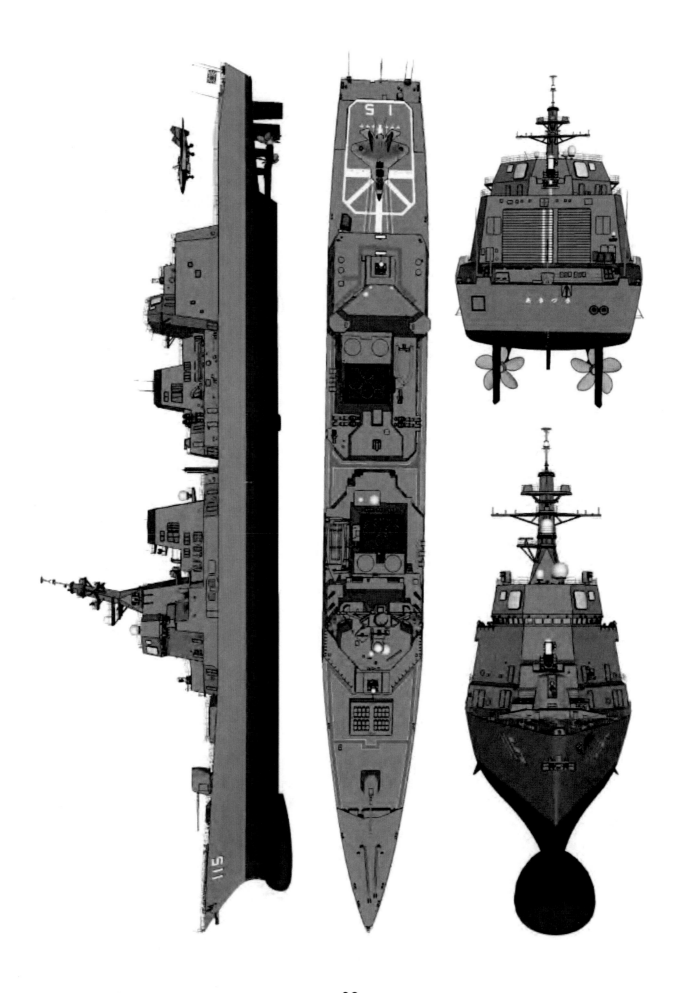

DD-115   JS Akizuki Destroyer

Japanese Name	秋月 (Autumn Moon)		
Type (Class)	Akizuki-class destroyer		
Commissioned	Mar 2012		
Length (meters)	150.5	**Crew**	230
Width (meters)	18.3	**Speed** (knots)	30
Draft (meters)	5.3	**Range** (nmi)	4,500 at 20 knots
Displacement (tons)			
Standard	5,000	**Fully Loaded**	6,800
Propulsion	COGAG, two shafts, four Rolls Royce Spey SM1C turbines		
Weapons	8 × Type 90 SSM		
	1 × Mk 41 VLS (32cells)		
	RIM-162 ESSM SAM		
	RUM-139 VL-ASROC		
	1 × 127mm (5 in)/54 gun		
	2 × 20mm Phalanx Block1B CIWS		
	2 × HOS-303 triple 324 mm (12.8 in) torpedo tubes		
Aircraft	1 × SH-60K Sea Hawk helicopter		

DD-116　　JS Teruzuki Destroyer

Japanese Name	照月 (Bright Moon)		
Type (Class)	Akizuki-class destroyer		
Commissioned	Mar 2013		
Length (meters)	150.5	**Crew**	230
Width (meters)	18.3	**Speed** (knots)	30
Draft (meters)	5.3	**Range** (nmi)	4,500 at 20 knots

Displacement (tons)

Standard	5,000	**Fully Loaded**	6,800

Propulsion	COGAG, two shafts, four Rolls Royce Spey SM1C turbines
Weapons	8 × Type 90 SSM
	1 × Mk 41 VLS (32cells)
	RIM-162 ESSM SAM
	Type 07 VL-ASROC
	1 × 127mm (5 in)/54 gun
	2 × 20mm Phalanx Block1B CIWS
	2 × HOS-303 triple 324 mm (12.8 in) torpedo tubes
Aircraft	1 × SH-60K Sea Hawk helicopter

DD-117   JS Suzutsuki Destroyer

Japanese Name	鈴月 (Clear Moon)		
Type (Class)	Akizuki-class destroyer		
Commissioned	Mar 2014		
Length (meters)	150.5	**Crew**	230
Width (meters)	18.3	**Speed** (knots)	30
Draft (meters)	5.3	**Range** (nmi)	4,500 at 20 knots
Displacement (tons)			
Standard	5,000	**Fully Loaded**	6,800
Propulsion	COGAG, two shafts, four Rolls Royce Spey SM1C turbines		
Weapons	8 × Type 90 SSM		
	1 × Mk 41 VLS (32cells)		
	RIM-162 ESSM SAM		
	Type 07 VL-ASROC		
	1 × 127mm (5 in)/54 gun		
	2 × 20mm Phalanx Block1B CIWS		
	2 × HOS-303 triple 324 mm (12.8 in) torpedo tubes		
Aircraft	1 × SH-60K Sea Hawk helicopter		

DD-118   JS Fuyuzuki Destroyer

海上自衛隊 / Japan Maritime Self-Defense Force

Japanese Name	冬月 (Winter Moon)		
Type (Class)	Akizuki-class destroyer		
Commissioned	Mar 2014		
Length (meters)	150.5	**Crew**	230
Width (meters)	18.3	**Speed** (knots)	30
Draft (meters)	5.3	**Range** (nmi)	4,500 at 20 knots
Displacement (tons)			
Standard	5,000	**Fully Loaded**	6,800
Propulsion	COGAG, two shafts, four Rolls Royce Spey SM1C turbines		
Weapons	8 × Type 90 SSM		
	1 × Mk 41 VLS (32cells)		
	RIM-162 ESSM SAM		
	Type 07 VL-ASROC		
	1 × 127mm (5 in)/54 gun		
	2 × 20mm Phalanx Block1B CIWS		
	2 × HOS-303 triple 324 mm (12.8 in) torpedo tubes		
Aircraft	1 × SH-60K Sea Hawk helicopter		

Takanami-Class Destroyers

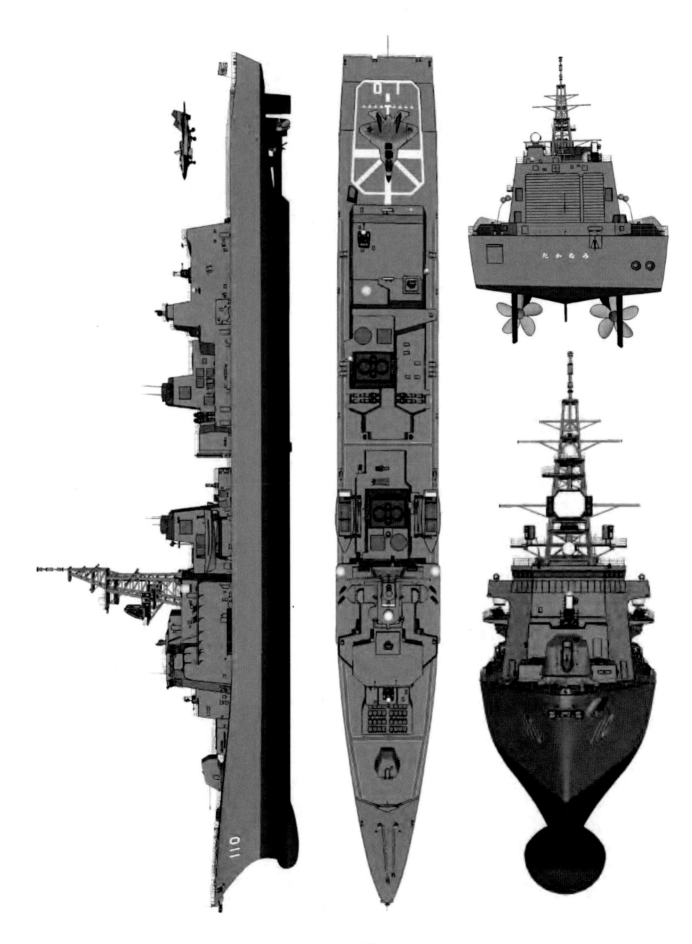

DD-110   JS Takanami Destroyer

Photo: Kenichiro Matohara CC BY 2.0

Japanese Name	たかなみ (Tall Waves)		
Type (Class)	Takanami-class destroyer		
Commissioned	Mar 2003		
Length (meters)	150.5	**Crew**	165
Width (meters)	17.4	**Speed** (knots)	30
Draft (meters)	5.2	**Range** (nmi)	

Displacement (tons)

Standard	4,650	**Fully Loaded**	6,300

Propulsion 2 × IHI-GE LM2500 gas turbines
2 × KHI-Rolls Royce Spey SM1C gas turbines
60,000 shp (45 MW)
2 shafts, cp props

Weapons 1 × Otobreda 127 mm/54 gun
2 × missile canister up to 8 Type 90 (SSM-1B)
2 × 20 mm Phalanx CIWS
2 × Type 68 triple torpedo tubes
VLS Mk 41 (32 cells)
  • Evolved Sea Sparrow SAM
  • RUM-139 VL ASROC

Aircraft 1 × SH-60J(K) Sea Hawk helicopter

DD-111   JS Onami Destroyer

Photo: 蚊注射

Japanese Name	おおなみ (Large Wave)		
Type (Class)	Takanami-class destroyer		
Commissioned	Mar 2003		
Length (meters)	151	**Crew**	175
Width (meters)	17.4	**Speed** (knots)	30
Draft (meters)	5.3	**Range** (nmi)	
Displacement (tons)			
Standard	4,650	**Fully Loaded**	6,300

Propulsion   2 × Ishikawajima Harima LM2500 gas turbines
2 × KHI-Rolls Royce Spey SM1C gas turbines
60,000 shp (45 MW)
2 shafts, cp props

Weapons   1 × Otobreda 127 mm/54 gun
2 × missile canister up to 8 Type 90 (SSM-1B)
2 × 20 mm Phalanx CIWS
2 × Type 68 triple torpedo tubes
VLS Mk 41 (32 cells)
  • Evolved Sea Sparrow SAM
  • RUM-139 VL ASROC

Aircraft   1 × SH-60J(K) Sea Hawk helicopter

DD-112 JS Makinami Destroyer

Photo: U.S. Navy

Japanese Name	まきなみ (Rolling Wave)
Type (Class)	Takanami-class destroyer
Commissioned	Mar 2004

Length (meters)	151	**Crew**	175
Width (meters)	17.4	**Speed** (knots)	30
Draft (meters)	5.3	**Range** (nmi)	

Displacement (tons)

Standard	4,650	**Fully Loaded**	6,300

Propulsion	2 × Ishikawajima Harima LM2500 gas turbines
	2 × KHI-Rolls Royce Spey SM1C gas turbines
	60,000 shp (45 MW)
	2 shafts, cp props
Weapons	1 × Otobreda 127 mm/54 gun
	2 × missile canister up to 8 Type 90 (SSM-1B)
	2 × 20 mm Phalanx CIWS
	2 × Type 68 triple torpedo tubes
	VLS Mk 41 (32 cells)
	• Evolved Sea Sparrow SAM
	• RUM-139 VL ASROC
Aircraft	1 × SH-60J(K) Sea Hawk helicopter

DD-113   JS Sazanami Destroyer

Japanese Name	さざなみ (Ripples on the Water)		
Type (Class)	Takanami-class destroyer		
Commissioned	Feb 2005		
Length (meters)	151	**Crew**	175
Width (meters)	17.4	**Speed** (knots)	30
Draft (meters)	5.3	**Range** (nmi)	

Displacement (tons)

Standard	4,650	**Fully Loaded**	6,300

Propulsion 2 × Ishikawajima Harima LM2500 gas turbines
2 × KHI-Rolls Royce Spey SM1C gas turbines
60,000 shp (45 MW)
2 shafts, cp props

Weapons 1 × Otobreda 127 mm/54 gun
2 × missile canister up to 8 Type 90 (SSM-1B)
2 × 20 mm Phalanx CIWS
2 × Type 68 triple torpedo tubes
VLS Mk 41 (32 cells)
  • Evolved Sea Sparrow SAM
  • RUM-139 VL ASROC

Aircraft 1 × SH-60J(K) Sea Hawk helicopter

DD-114 JS Suzunami Destroyer

Photo: hygeta CCA 2.1

Japanese Name	すずなみ (Breaking Waves)		
Type (Class)	Takanami-class destroyer		
Commissioned	Feb 2006		
Length (meters)	151	**Crew**	175
Width (meters)	17.4	**Speed** (knots)	30
Draft (meters)	5.3	**Range** (nmi)	
Displacement (tons)			
Standard	4,650	**Fully Loaded**	6,300
Propulsion	2 × Ishikawajima Harima LM2500 gas turbines		
	2 × KHI-Rolls Royce Spey SM1C gas turbines		
	60,000 shp (45 MW)		
	2 shafts, cp props		
Weapons	1 × Otobreda 127 mm/54 gun		
	2 × missile canister up to 8 Type 90 (SSM-1B)		
	2 × 20 mm Phalanx CIWS		
	2 × Type 68 triple torpedo tubes		
	VLS Mk 41 (32 cells)		
	• Evolved Sea Sparrow SAM		
	• RUM-139 VL ASROC		
Aircraft	1 × SH-60J(K) Sea Hawk helicopter		

47

Other books available on Amazon.com:

China Combat Submarines 2019-2020

Russia Combat Submarines 2019-2020

North Korea Combat Submarines 2019-2020

Iran Combat Submarines 2019-2020

Murasame-Class Destroyers

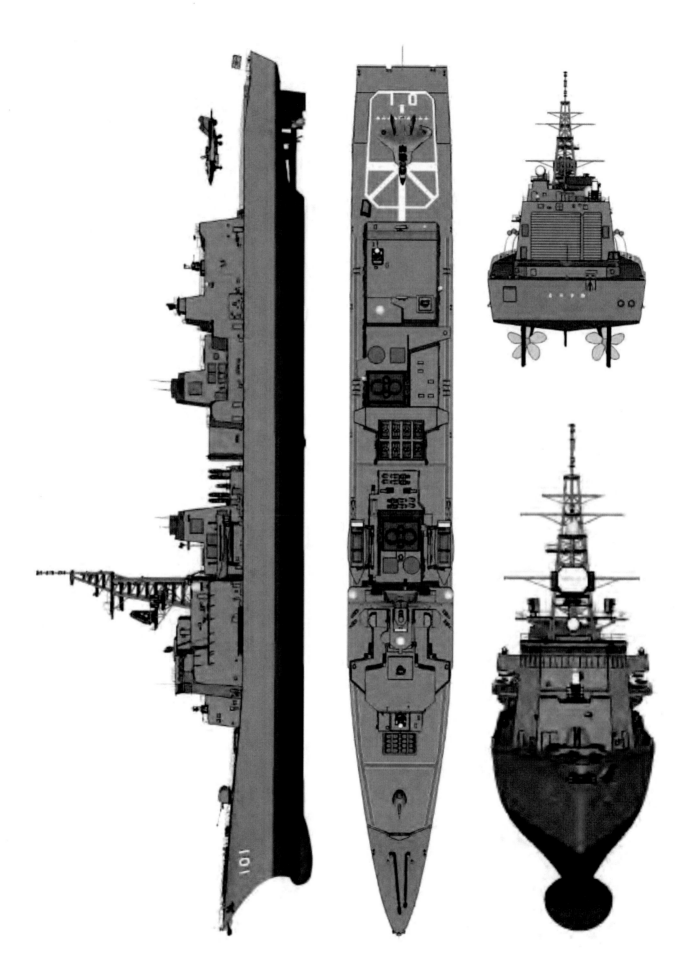

DD-101 JS Murasame Destroyer

Photo: Don S. Montgomery, U.S. Navy

Japanese Name	むらさめ型護衛艦 Murasame-gata-goei-kan (Village Rain)		
Type (Class)	Murasame-class destroyer		
Commissioned	Mar 1996		
Length (meters)	151	**Crew**	155
Width (meters)	17.4	**Speed** (knots)	30
Draft (meters)	5.2	**Range** (nmi)	

Displacement (tons)

Standard	4,550	**Fully Loaded**	6,200

Propulsion	2 × Ishikawajima Harima LM2500 gas turbines
	2 × KHI-Rolls Royce Spey SM1C gas turbines
	60,000 shp (45 MW)
	2 shafts, cp props
Weapons	1 × OTO Melara 76 mm gun
	2 × 20 mm Phalanx CIWS
	2 × SSM-1B quad canisters
	2 × triple 324 mm torpedo tubes
	VLS Mk 48 (16 cells)
	• Evolved Sea Sparrow SAM
	VLS Mk 41 (16 cells)
	• VL-ASROC
Aircraft	1 × SH-60J(K) Sea Hawk anti-submarine helicopter

DD-102   JS Harusame Destroyer

Photo: Jeremie Yoder, U.S. Navy

Japanese Name	春雨 (Spring Rain)
Type (Class)	Murasame-class destroyer
Commissioned	Mar 1997

Length (meters)	151	**Crew**	155
Width (meters)	17.4	**Speed** (knots)	30
Draft (meters)	5.2	**Range** (nmi)	

Displacement (tons)

Standard	4,550	**Fully Loaded**	6,200

Propulsion	2 × Ishikawajima Harima LM2500 gas turbines
	2 × KHI-Rolls Royce Spey SM1C gas turbines
	60,000 shp (45 MW)
	2 shafts, cp props
Weapons	1 × OTO Melara 76 mm gun
	2 × 20 mm Phalanx CIWS
	2 × SSM-1B quad canisters
	2 × triple 324 mm torpedo tubes
	VLS Mk 48 (16 cells)
	• Evolved Sea Sparrow SAM
	VLS Mk 41 (16 cells)
	• VL-ASROC
Aircraft	1 × SH-60J(K) Sea Hawk anti-submarine helicopter

DD-103   JS Yudachi Destroyer

Photo: Don S. Montgomery, U.S. Navy

Japanese Name	ゆだち (Evening Downpour)
Type (Class)	Murasame-class destroyer
Commissioned	Mar 1999

Length (meters)	151	**Crew**	155
Width (meters)	17.4	**Speed** (knots)	30
Draft (meters)	5.2	**Range** (nmi)	

Displacement (tons)

Standard	4,550	**Fully Loaded**	6,200

Propulsion	2 × Ishikawajima Harima LM2500 gas turbines
	2 × KHI-Rolls Royce Spey SM1C gas turbines
	60,000 shp (45 MW)
	2 shafts, cp props
Weapons	1 × OTO Melara 76 mm gun
	2 × 20 mm Phalanx CIWS
	2 × SSM-1B quad canisters
	2 × triple 324 mm torpedo tubes
	VLS Mk 48 (16 cells)
	• Evolved Sea Sparrow SAM
	VLS Mk 41 (16 cells)
	• VL-ASROC
Aircraft	1 × SH-60J(K) Sea Hawk anti-submarine helicopter

DD-104   JS Kirisame Destroyer

Photo: Don S. Montgomery, U.S. Navy

Japanese Name	きりさめ (Drizzle)		
Type (Class)	Murasame-class destroyer		
Commissioned	Mar 1999		
Length (meters)	151	**Crew**	155
Width (meters)	17.4	**Speed** (knots)	30
Draft (meters)	5.2	**Range** (nmi)	
Displacement (tons)			
Standard	4,550	**Fully Loaded**	6,200
Propulsion	2 × Ishikawajima Harima LM2500 gas turbines		
	2 × KHI-Rolls Royce Spey SM1C gas turbines		
	60,000 shp (45 MW)		
	2 shafts, cp props		
Weapons	1 × OTO Melara 76 mm gun		
	2 × 20 mm Phalanx CIWS		
	2 × SSM-1B quad canisters		
	2 × triple 324 mm torpedo tubes		
	VLS Mk 48 (16 cells)		
	• Evolved Sea Sparrow SAM		
	VLS Mk 41 (16 cells)		
	• VL-ASROC		
Aircraft	1 × SH-60J(K) Sea Hawk anti-submarine helicopter		

DD-105   JS Inazuma Destroyer

Photo: James E. Foehl, U.S. Navy

Japanese Name	イナズマ (Sudden Lightning)		
Type (Class)	Murasame-class destroyer		
Commissioned	Mar 2000		
Length (meters)	151	**Crew**	155
Width (meters)	17.4	**Speed** (knots)	30
Draft (meters)	5.2	**Range** (nmi)	
Displacement (tons)			
Standard	4,550	**Fully Loaded**	6,200
Propulsion	2 × Ishikawajima Harima LM2500 gas turbines		
	2 × KHI-Rolls Royce Spey SM1C gas turbines		
	60,000 shp (45 MW)		
	2 shafts, cp props		
Weapons	1 × OTO Melara 76 mm gun		
	2 × 20 mm Phalanx CIWS		
	2 × SSM-1B quad canisters		
	2 × triple 324 mm torpedo tubes		
	VLS Mk 48 (16 cells)		
	• Evolved Sea Sparrow SAM		
	VLS Mk 41 (16 cells)		
	• VL-ASROC		
Aircraft	1 × SH-60J(K) Sea Hawk anti-submarine helicopter		

DD-106   JS Samidare Destroyer

Photo: Rebecca J. Moat, U.S. Navy

Japanese Name	さみだれ (Poetic term for the Rainy Season)		
Type (Class)	Murasame-class destroyer		
Commissioned	Mar 2000		
Length (meters)	151	**Crew**	155
Width (meters)	17.4	**Speed** (knots)	30
Draft (meters)	5.2	**Range** (nmi)	
Displacement (tons)			
Standard	4,550	**Fully Loaded**	6,200
Propulsion	2 × Ishikawajima Harima LM2500 gas turbines		
	2 × KHI-Rolls Royce Spey SM1C gas turbines		
	60,000 shp (45 MW)		
	2 shafts, cp props		
Weapons	1 × OTO Melara 76 mm gun		
	2 × 20 mm Phalanx CIWS		
	2 × SSM-1B quad canisters		
	2 × triple 324 mm torpedo tubes		
	VLS Mk 48 (16 cells)		
	• Evolved Sea Sparrow SAM		
	VLS Mk 41 (16 cells)		
	• VL-ASROC		
Aircraft	1 × SH-60J(K) Sea Hawk anti-submarine helicopter		

DD-107   JS Ikazuchi Destroyer

Japanese Name	イカヅチ (Ferocious Thunder)
Type (Class)	Murasame-class destroyer
Commissioned	Mar 2001

Length (meters)	151	**Crew**	155
Width (meters)	17.4	**Speed** (knots)	30
Draft (meters)	5.2	**Range** (nmi)	

Displacement (tons)

Standard	4,550	**Fully Loaded**	6,200

Propulsion	2 × Ishikawajima Harima LM2500 gas turbines
	2 × KHI-Rolls Royce Spey SM1C gas turbines
	60,000 shp (45 MW)
	2 shafts, cp props
Weapons	1 × OTO Melara 76 mm gun
	2 × 20 mm Phalanx CIWS
	2 × SSM-1B quad canisters
	2 × triple 324 mm torpedo tubes
	VLS Mk 48 (16 cells)
	• Evolved Sea Sparrow SAM
	VLS Mk 41 (16 cells)
	• VL-ASROC
Aircraft	1 × SH-60J(K) Sea Hawk anti-submarine helicopter

DD-108   JS Akebono Destroyer

海上自衛隊 / Japan Maritime Self-Defense Force

Japanese Name	あけぼの (Light of Daybreak)		
Type (Class)	Murasame-class destroyer		
Commissioned	Mar 2002		
Length (meters)	151	**Crew**	155
Width (meters)	17.4	**Speed** (knots)	30
Draft (meters)	5.2	**Range** (nmi)	

Displacement (tons)

Standard	4,550	**Fully Loaded**	6,200

Propulsion
2 × Ishikawajima Harima LM2500 gas turbines
2 × KHI-Rolls Royce Spey SM1C gas turbines
60,000 shp (45 MW)
2 shafts, cp props

Weapons
1 × OTO Melara 76 mm gun
2 × 20 mm Phalanx CIWS
2 × SSM-1B quad canisters
2 × triple 324 mm torpedo tubes
VLS Mk 48 (16 cells)
 • Evolved Sea Sparrow SAM
VLS Mk 41 (16 cells)
 • VL-ASROC

Aircraft
1 × SH-60J(K) Sea Hawk anti-submarine helicopter

DD-109   JS Ariake Destroyer

Photo: Todd Frantom, U.S. Navy

Japanese Name	有明 (Daybreak)		
Type (Class)	Murasame-class destroyer		
Commissioned	Mar 2002		
Length (meters)	151	**Crew**	155
Width (meters)	17.4	**Speed** (knots)	30
Draft (meters)	5.2	**Range** (nmi)	
Displacement (tons)			
Standard	4,550	**Fully Loaded**	6,200
Propulsion	2 × Ishikawajima Harima LM2500 gas turbines		
	2 × KHI-Rolls Royce Spey SM1C gas turbines		
	60,000 shp (45 MW)		
	2 shafts, cp props		
Weapons	1 × OTO Melara 76 mm gun		
	2 × 20 mm Phalanx CIWS		
	2 × SSM-1B quad canisters		
	2 × triple 324 mm torpedo tubes		
	VLS Mk 48 (16 cells)		
	• Evolved Sea Sparrow SAM		
	VLS Mk 41 (16 cells)		
	• VL-ASROC		
Aircraft	1 × SH-60J(K) Sea Hawk anti-submarine helicopter		

Other books available on Amazon.com:

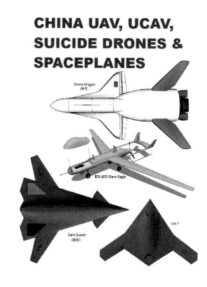

Small Destroyers

Asagiri-Class Destroyers

3D model by: Sir Topham hatt

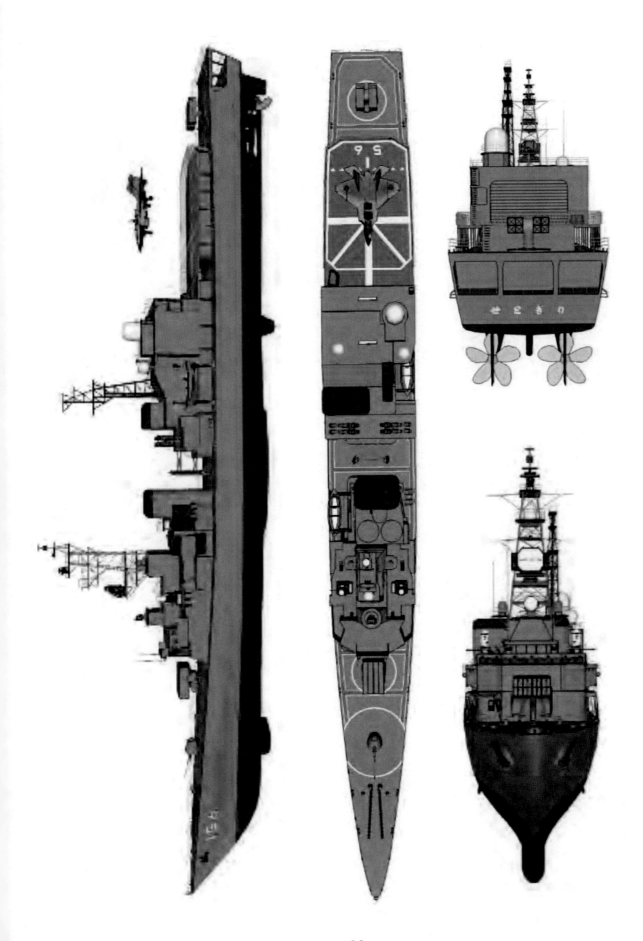

DD-151   JS Asagiri Destroyer

Photo: John Bouvia, U.S. Navy

Japanese Name	あさぎり型護衛艦 (Asagiri-gata-goei-kan)		
Type (Class)	Asagiri-class destroyer		
Commissioned	1988		
Length (meters)	137	**Crew**	220
Width (meters)	14.6	**Speed** (knots)	30
Draft (meters)	4.5	**Range** (nmi)	6,000
Displacement (tons)			
Standard	3,500	**Fully Loaded**	5,200
Propulsion	4 × KHI-RR SM1A gas turbines 54,000 shp (40 MW)		
	2 shafts, cp props		
Weapons	1 × OTO Melara 76 mm gun		
	2 × 20 mm Phalanx CIWS		
	2 × Harpoon SSM quad canisters		
	1 × Sea Sparrow SAM octuple launcher		
	1 × ASROC octuple launcher		
	2 × triple 324 mm (12.8 in) torpedo tubes		
Aircraft	1 × SH-60J(K) Sea Hawk anti-submarine helicopter		

DD-152   JS Yamagiri Destroyer

Photo: John Bouvia, U.S. Navy

Japanese Name	やまぎり		
Type (Class)	Asagiri-class destroyer		
Commissioned	1989		
Length (meters)	137	**Crew**	220
Width (meters)	14.6	**Speed** (knots)	30
Draft (meters)	4.5	**Range** (nmi)	6,000
Displacement (tons)			
Standard	3,500	**Fully Loaded**	5,200
Propulsion	4 × KHI-RR SM1A gas turbines 54,000 shp (40 MW)		
	2 shafts, cp props		
Weapons	1 × OTO Melara 76 mm gun		
	2 × 20 mm Phalanx CIWS		
	2 × Harpoon SSM quad canisters		
	1 × Sea Sparrow SAM octuple launcher		
	1 × ASROC octuple launcher		
	2 × triple 324 mm (12.8 in) torpedo tubes		
Aircraft	1 × SH-60J(K) Sea Hawk anti-submarine helicopter		

DD-153   JS Yūgiri Destroyer

Japanese Name	夕霧		
Type (Class)	Asagiri-class destroyer		
Commissioned	1989		
Length (meters)	137	**Crew**	220
Width (meters)	14.6	**Speed** (knots)	30
Draft (meters)	4.5	**Range** (nmi)	6,000
Displacement (tons)			
Standard	3,500	**Fully Loaded**	5,200
Propulsion	4 × KHI-RR SM1A gas turbines 54,000 shp (40 MW)		
	2 shafts, cp props		
Weapons	1 × OTO Melara 76 mm gun		
	2 × 20 mm Phalanx CIWS		
	2 × Harpoon SSM quad canisters		
	1 × Sea Sparrow SAM octuple launcher		
	1 × ASROC octuple launcher		
	2 × triple 324 mm (12.8 in) torpedo tubcs		
Aircraft	1 × SH-60J(K) Sea Hawk anti-submarine helicopter		

DD-154　　　JS Amagiri Destroyer

Photo: Richard J. Brunson, U.S. Navy

Japanese Name	天霧
Type (Class)	Asagiri-class destroyer
Commissioned	Feb 1989

Length (meters)	137	**Crew**	220
Width (meters)	14.6	**Speed** (knots)	30
Draft (meters)	4.5	**Range** (nmi)	6,000

Displacement (tons)

Standard	3,500	**Fully Loaded**	5,200

Propulsion	4 × KHI-RR SM1A gas turbines 54,000 shp (40 MW)
	2 shafts, cp props
Weapons	1 × OTO Melara 76 mm gun
	2 × 20 mm Phalanx CIWS
	2 × Harpoon SSM quad canisters
	1 × Sea Sparrow SAM octuple launcher
	1 × ASROC octuple launcher
	2 × triple 324 mm (12.8 in) torpedo tubes
Aircraft	1 × SH-60J(K) Sea Hawk anti-submarine helicopter

DD-155   JS Hamagiri Destroyer

Photo: Don Bray, U.S. Navy

Japanese Name	はまぎり		
Type (Class)	Asagiri-class destroyer		
Commissioned	1990		
Length (meters)	137	**Crew**	220
Width (meters)	14.6	**Speed** (knots)	30
Draft (meters)	4.5	**Range** (nmi)	6,000
Displacement (tons)			
Standard	3,500	**Fully Loaded**	5,200
Propulsion	4 × KHI-RR SM1A gas turbines 54,000 shp (40 MW)		
	2 shafts, cp props		
Weapons	1 × OTO Melara 76 mm gun		
	2 × 20 mm Phalanx CIWS		
	2 × Harpoon SSM quad canisters		
	1 × Sea Sparrow SAM octuple launcher		
	1 × ASROC octuple launcher		
	2 × triple 324 mm (12.8 in) torpedo tubes		
Aircraft	1 × SH-60J(K) Sea Hawk anti-submarine helicopter		

DD-156   JS Setogiri Destroyer

Photo: Ka23 13

Japanese Name	瀬戸切		
Type (Class)	Asagiri-class destroyer		
Commissioned	1990		
Length (meters)	137	**Crew**	220
Width (meters)	14.6	**Speed** (knots)	30
Draft (meters)	4.5	**Range** (nmi)	6,000
Displacement (tons)			
Standard	3,500	**Fully Loaded**	5,200
Propulsion	4 × KHI-RR SM1A gas turbines 54,000 shp (40 MW)		
	2 shafts, cp props		
Weapons	1 × OTO Melara 76 mm gun		
	2 × 20 mm Phalanx CIWS		
	2 × Harpoon SSM quad canisters		
	1 × Sea Sparrow SAM octuple launcher		
	1 × ASROC octuple launcher		
	2 × triple 324 mm (12.8 in) torpedo tubes		
Aircraft	1 × SH-60J(K) Sea Hawk anti-submarine helicopter		

Photo: Walter Pels, U.S. Navy

DD-157   JS Sawagiri Destroyer

Photo: Fwng3431

Japanese Name	さわぎり		
Type (Class)	Asagiri-class destroyer		
Commissioned	1990		
Length (meters)	137	**Crew**	220
Width (meters)	14.6	**Speed** (knots)	30
Draft (meters)	4.5	**Range** (nmi)	6,000
Displacement (tons)			
Standard	3,500	**Fully Loaded**	5,200
Propulsion	4 × KHI-RR SM1A gas turbines 54,000 shp (40 MW)		
	2 shafts, cp props		
Weapons	1 × OTO Melara 76 mm gun		
	2 × 20 mm Phalanx CIWS		
	2 × Harpoon SSM quad canisters		
	1 × Sea Sparrow SAM octuple launcher		
	1 × ASROC octuple launcher		
	2 × triple 324 mm (12.8 in) torpedo tubes		
Aircraft	1 × SH-60J(K) Sea Hawk anti-submarine helicopter		

DD-158   JS Umigiri Destroyer

Photo: Kenichiro MATOHARA, CCA 2.0

Japanese Name	うみぎり
Type (Class)	Asagiri-class destroyer
Commissioned	1991

Length (meters)	137	**Crew**	220
Width (meters)	14.6	**Speed** (knots)	30
Draft (meters)	4.5	**Range** (nmi)	6,000

Displacement (tons)

Standard	3,500	**Fully Loaded**	5,200

Propulsion	4 × KHI-RR SM1A gas turbines 54,000 shp (40 MW)
	2 shafts, cp props
Weapons	1 × OTO Melara 76 mm gun
	2 × 20 mm Phalanx CIWS
	2 × Harpoon SSM quad canisters
	1 × Sea Sparrow SAM octuple launcher
	1 × ASROC octuple launcher
	2 × triple 324 mm (12.8 in) torpedo tubes
Aircraft	1 × SH-60J(K) Sea Hawk anti-submarine helicopter

Hatsuyuki-Class Destroyers

DD-130   JS Matsuyuki Destroyer

Japanese Name	うみぎり		
Type (Class)	Hatsuyuki-class destroyer		
Commissioned	Mar 1986		
Length (meters)	130	**Crew**	220
Width (meters)	14.6	**Speed** (knots)	30
Draft (meters)	4.5	**Range** (nmi)	6,000
Displacement (tons)			
Standard	3,500	**Fully Loaded**	5,200
Propulsion	4 × KHI-RR SM1A gas turbines 54,000 shp (40 MW)		
	2 shafts, cp props		
Weapons	1 × OTO Melara 76 mm gun		
	2 × 20 mm Phalanx CIWS		
	2 × Harpoon SSM quad canisters		
	1 × Sea Sparrow SAM octuple launcher		
	1 × ASROC octuple launcher		
	2 × triple 324 mm (12.8 in) torpedo tubes		
Aircraft	1 × SH-60J(K) Sea Hawk anti-submarine helicopter		

DD-132   JS Asayuki Destroyer

海上自衛隊 / Japan Maritime Self-Defense Force

Japanese Name	あさゆき		
Type (Class)	Hatsuyuki-class destroyer		
Commissioned	Mar 1987		
Length (meters)	130	**Crew**	220
Width (meters)	14.6	**Speed** (knots)	30
Draft (meters)	4.5	**Range** (nmi)	6,000
Displacement (tons)			
Standard	3,500	**Fully Loaded**	5,200
Propulsion	4 × KHI-RR SM1A gas turbines 54,000 shp (40 MW) 2 shafts, cp props		
Weapons	1 × OTO Melara 76 mm gun 2 × 20 mm Phalanx CIWS 2 × Harpoon SSM quad canisters 1 × Sea Sparrow SAM octuple launcher 1 × ASROC octuple launcher 2 × triple 324 mm (12.8 in) torpedo tubes		
Aircraft	1 × SH-60J(K) Sea Hawk anti-submarine helicopter		

Ōsumi-Class Landing Ship Tanks

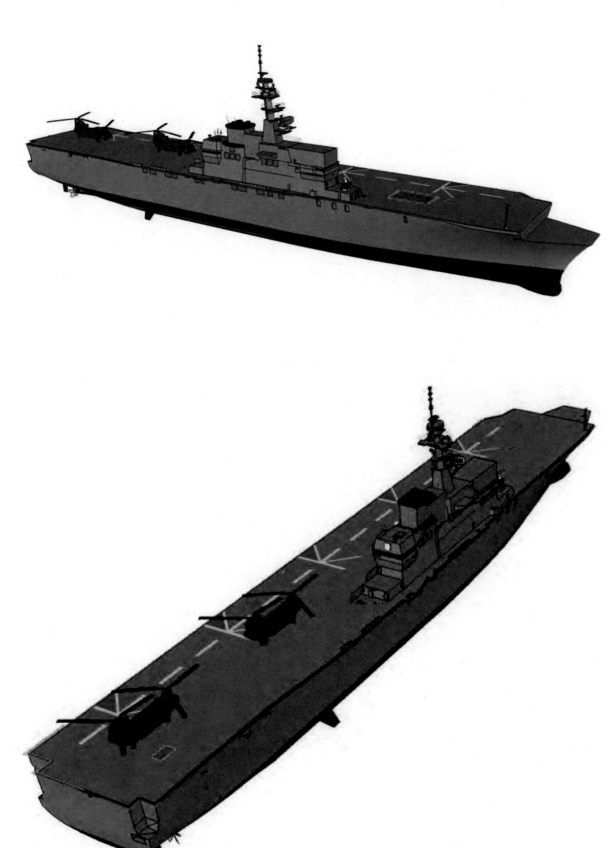

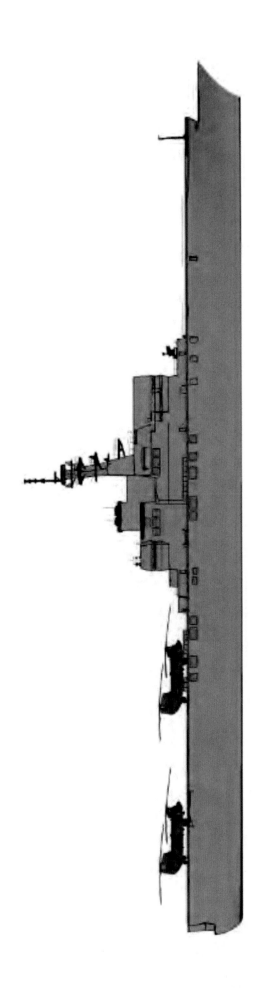

LST 4001   JS Ōsumi Landing Ship Tank

Photo: Ogiyoshisan CCA 4.0

Japanese Name	大隅 (Finished)		
Type (Class)	Ōsumi-class Landing Ship Tank		
Commissioned	Mar 1998		
Length (meters)	178	**Crew**	138 +330 troops
Width (meters)	25.8	**Speed** (knots)	22
Draft (meters)	17	**Range** (nmi)	

Displacement (tons)

Standard	8,900	**Fully Loaded**	14,000

Propulsion	2 × Mitsui 16V42M-A Diesel (2 shafts propulsion, 26,000 bhp.)
	1 × bow thruster
Weapons	2 × 20 mm Phalanx CIWS
	2 × 12.7mm machine gun M2
Aircraft	Up to 8 helicopters
Note:	Two Landing Craft Air Cushion (LCAC)
	Troops: 330/1000 long/short duration
	up to 10 main battle tanks

海上自衛隊 / Japan Maritime Self-Defense Force

LST 4002   JS Shimokita Landing Ship Tank

Photo: Patrick Dionne, U.S. Navy

Japanese Name	下北
Type (Class)	Ōsumi-class Landing Ship Tank
Commissioned	Mar 2002

Length (meters)	178	**Crew**	138 +330 troops
Width (meters)	25.8	**Speed** (knots)	22
Draft (meters)	17	**Range** (nmi)	

Displacement (tons)

Standard	8,900	**Fully Loaded**	14,000

Propulsion	2 × Mitsui 16V42M-A Diesel (2 shafts propulsion, 26,000 bhp.)
	1 × bow thruster
Weapons	2 × 20 mm Phalanx CIWS
	2 × 12.7mm machine gun M2
Aircraft	Up to 8 helicopters
Note:	Two Landing Craft Air Cushion (LCAC)
	Troops: 330/1000 long/short duration
	up to 10 main battle tanks

LST 4003   JS Kunisaki Landing Ship Tank

海上自衛隊 / Japan Maritime Self-Defense Force

Japanese Name	国崎		
Type (Class)	Ōsumi-class Landing Ship Tank		
Commissioned	Feb 2003		
Length (meters)	178	**Crew**	138 +330 troops
Width (meters)	25.8	**Speed** (knots)	22
Draft (meters)	17	**Range** (nmi)	
Displacement (tons)			
Standard	8,900	**Fully Loaded**	14,000
Propulsion	2 × Mitsui 16V42M-A Diesel (2 shafts propulsion, 26,000 bhp.)		
	1 × bow thruster		
Weapons	2 × 20 mm Phalanx CIWS		
	2 × 12.7mm machine gun M2		
Aircraft	Up to 8 helicopters		
Note:	Two Landing Craft Air Cushion (LCAC)		
	Troops: 330/1000 long/short duration		
	up to 10 main battle tanks		

Made in the USA
Middletown, DE
21 January 2022